LAUGH OFTEN

and More Great
Advice from
the Bible

written by
HANOCH PIVEN
and **SHIRA
HECHT-KOLLER**

illustrated by Hanoch Piven
text written with Naomi Shulman

Farrar Straus Giroux
New York

In this book, you'll get to meet some of the most famous characters from the Bible: Abraham and Sarah, Moses and Miriam, David and Goliath. Maybe you recognize a few of these names already. You will also meet characters who may be new to you, like Deborah, Elijah, and Balaam.

Even though the stories of the Bible are very old, there is still a lot that we can learn from each of these characters. We can imagine what advice they might have offered us, had we been given the chance to meet them.

This book is about paying attention not just to the words on the page but also to the objects that compose the illustrations. The artwork might even tell more than what is written. Each story may send you on a research quest to learn more about these figures, or prompt you to imagine your own alternative stories.

Paying attention to details and exploring what they mean is what studying the Bible is all about.

EVE

Be Curious

"Look at the tree of knowledge," the snake said to Eve. "Doesn't its fruit look beautiful?"

Everything was beautiful and perfect in the Garden of Eden. After all, it was brand-new.

Eve *herself* was new, and the more she learned about this new world, the more she wanted to know. She turned over every rock and petted every animal. So when she came to the tree of knowledge, of course she wanted to taste its fruit. But that wasn't just against the rules—it was FORBIDDEN.

"Go ahead," hissed the snake. "Have a nibble. I won't tell." Eve looked to the left and she looked to the right—and then she took a bite.

Upon first taste, Eve realized that the world was more complicated than it had seemed. Once you know something, you can't unknow it.

But the world was still beautiful. And she was curious to know even more.

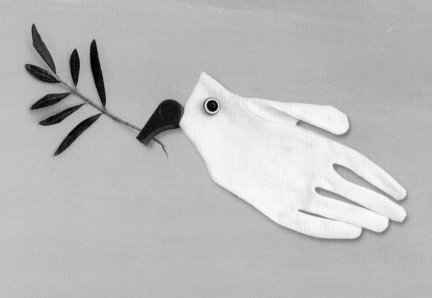

NOAH

Be Good

The world was beautiful but messy. People had polluted it with bad behavior. God decided to give it a good scrubbing.

God needed some help. Who better to help than Noah? The rest of the world may have needed washing, but Noah was clean as a whistle—inside and out.

God asked for Noah's help saving the wonderful creatures of the world. The animals happily boarded Noah's boat, two by two. With Noah at the helm, they knew they would be safe and cared for inside his ark. And that was a good thing.

ABRAHAM

Trust the Journey

Abraham just couldn't find his place in the world. He was puzzled by so many questions—questions that he didn't even know how to ask. He knew he needed answers. So he set out on a journey to find them.

Abraham started walking, trusting the road to take him where he needed to go. The road was long and twisting, and at times, he was hungry and frustrated. But with each new stop on the way, he grew rich— both in livestock and in friends. He was learning about the world and himself.

Abraham kept traveling to a ripe old age. When he finally settled down, he had become the father of a large family that would keep growing, eventually crossing the world the way the stars cross the sky.

It took Abraham a lifelong journey to solve the puzzle and find his place in the world.

SARAH

Laugh Yourself Silly

Sarah thought she'd seen and heard it all. And then, one day, three strangers came to visit. Nothing unusual about that. But after she and her husband, Abraham, welcomed them and fed them, the strangers told her she'd have a baby soon.

Sarah blushed. That was the silliest thing she'd ever heard. Couldn't they see how old she was? Much too old to have a baby! What could she possibly say? Sometimes there are no words. She just had to laugh.

And a year later, when she cuddled her baby, she laughed again. Isn't life funny? Oh, and by the way: The baby's name was Isaac—Hebrew for "one who laughs."

JOSEPH

Dream Big

Joseph had ten older brothers. That made it hard to find his place—both in his family and in the world. But he never had trouble fitting in when he was asleep. Some people dream in black and white, but for Joseph, dreams were a coat of many colors. His brothers teased him for being a dreamer, but Joseph didn't mind being different. When life presented problems, Joseph's dreams gave him the answers. And soon he realized he could help other people find answers in their dreams, too.

When Pharaoh, the king of Egypt, began having strange dreams, Joseph was the only one who could make sense of them. Pharaoh's dreams were not just dreams: They were warnings. Joseph helped Pharaoh interpret the messages and prepare for the challenges ahead.

Joseph showed that sometimes a dream can be more than a dream—it can lead to a new and better reality.

MIRIAM

Take Care

Moving quietly through the reeds, Miriam kept her gaze fixed on her brother Moses.

The family had kept Moses hidden from Pharaoh's cruel laws for as long as they could. Now they took a chance and set him adrift on the Nile River. Hidden along the riverbank, Miriam was paying close attention.

Pharaoh's daughter was delighted to find the baby in a basket. "I'll keep him," she said. This was Miriam's moment. She stepped out of the reeds and spoke: "I know someone who can look after him for you—my mother." And that's how Pharaoh's daughter hired Moses's own mother to care for him.

This baby would not be harmed. Not on Miriam's watch.

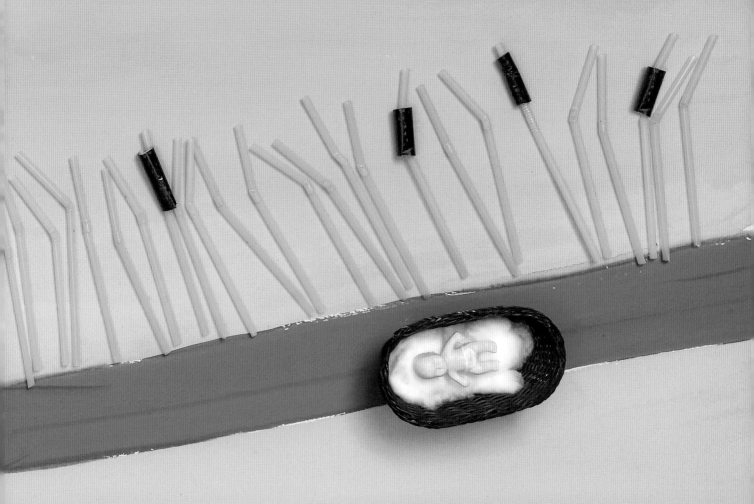

MOSES

Listen Up

Speaking didn't come easily to Moses. He stumbled over his words. But out in the desert, away from people, he was as sure-footed as the sheep he tended. Speaking meant nothing to the animals. In order to lead them, the trick was to *listen*. Was a lamb crying? Was danger lurking? To do his job right, Moses had to keep his mouth shut, and his eyes and ears open.

The day came when Moses needed to lead a different group through the desert—the people of Israel. At first, Moses wasn't sure he could do it. But a leader never runs from responsibility. And Moses soon realized that he already knew how to do this job.

Moses stepped up to lead. And the Israelites followed.

BALAAM

Learn from Animals

Balaam's donkey was very trusty. But one day, the donkey stopped short in the middle of the path. Balaam looked all around—he couldn't see anything blocking their way. Why wouldn't the animal move? Why was she being so stubborn?

Balaam went berserk! He shouted mean words. He shouted and shouted until the donkey just couldn't stand it. Somebody needed to stop Balaam, so the donkey spoke up.

"Pardon me," the donkey said. "Could you stop yelling? You're being very rude."

Now Balaam *really* went berserk. "What?!" shouted Balaam. "A talking donkey?!"

"Am I not your trusty donkey? Have I ever steered you off course?" she replied. "Do you not see there is an angel in our path?"

And only when Balaam shut his mouth was he able to open his eyes—and see what the donkey saw.

DEBORAH

Feel Your Power

Back in Deborah's day, most judges were men. But all who knew Deborah looked to her to judge their struggles. She was wise. She understood that fair was fair. People trusted her.

Even General Barak took his army to battle because Deborah told him to. "But on one condition," he told her. "You come, too. I'm afraid to go without you."

Back in Deborah's day, most soldiers were men. But Barak felt Deborah's power, and Deborah felt it, too. She arose from her perch beneath a palm tree and headed into battle with Barak.

Deborah's fiery determination lit up the battlefield, and the Israelites won, lighting the way for powerful men—and women—to follow.

DAVID

Be Yourself

David the shepherd wasn't big or strong, but he walked with confidence. His sheep were happy and healthy as could be. That's because David was smart and kind. He was also an ace with a slingshot: His aim was always true. He was comfortable being himself.

When the giant Goliath came looking for a fight, he seemed unbeatable. So tall. So big! All the things David wasn't. Everyone thought David was no match for Goliath.

But David knew he didn't have to be Goliath. He just had to be David. And he knew he had at least one talent that Goliath did not have. He smiled and lifted his slingshot.

His aim was true.

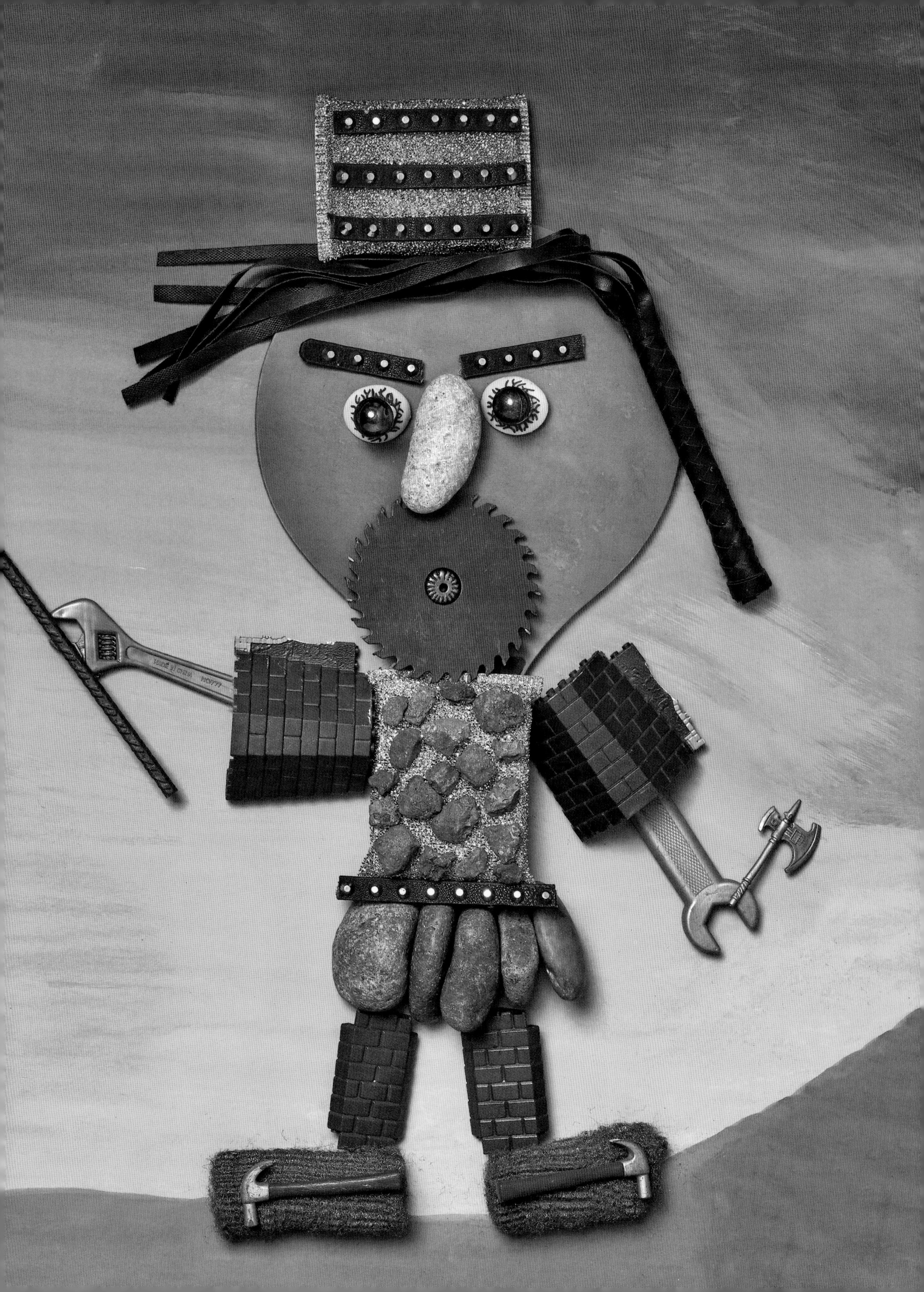

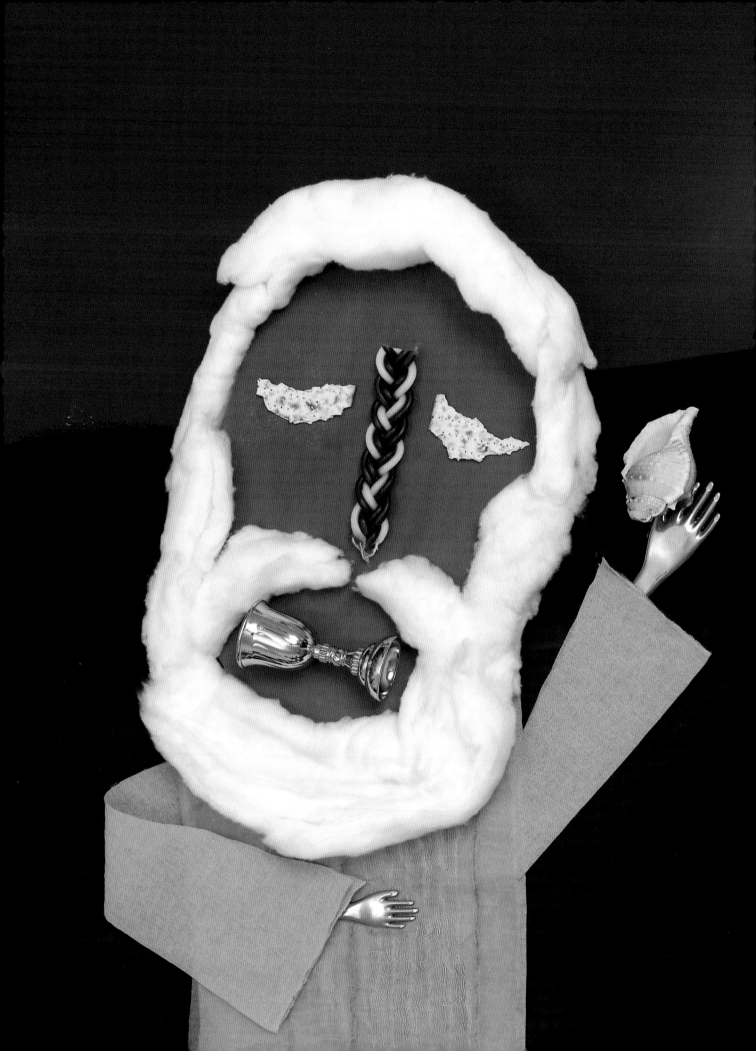

ELIJAH

Find the Quiet

Elijah's world was full of noise and drama. Lightning filled the sky, fires scorched the earth, and people thundered at one another, too. Elijah had a good part in creating all that. He simply loved a good spectacle. The more fires and explosions, the better! Or so he thought.

But with all that noise, Elijah's life was a constant roller coaster. He was often angry and sometimes scared.

Finally, Elijah had had enough noise. He crawled into a cave, then climbed to the top of a mountain. But even there, wind crashed against rocks, thunder blasted his ears, and fire raged around him.

Elijah stood still. And listened.

In the eye of the storm, a silence fell. Elijah heard a still, small voice—and he knew it was more truthful than any loud thunder.

JONAH

Take a Time-Out

Jonah was thrown overboard into the sea.

Why? He tried to run from his responsibility. But Jonah was not alone. A huge fish scooped Jonah up and swallowed him, rescuing him from the ocean, and there Jonah sat, in its belly, for three days—long enough to think about what he had done.

A little "alone time" was exactly what Jonah needed in order to reconsider. Sometimes our first response isn't the right one.

After three days of thinking, Jonah knew what he had to do and was ready to do it. So the fish let Jonah go.

(Guess what? It wasn't the last time Jonah needed a time-out.)

RUTH

Find Your People

Ruth was open to adventure. She married an outsider from a faraway land and moved in with his family. Ruth loved her mother-in-law, Naomi. Life was sweet.

But then Ruth's husband died, a famine made life bitter, and everyone grew hungry. Suddenly, she and Naomi were forced to gather fallen wheat in the field.

It was no use. "Go," Naomi said to Ruth. "Return to your home. Go to a place where life will be easier for you."

But Ruth refused. After all, when life is bitter, it's being with people you love that adds sweetness. "Where you go, I will go," Ruth said. "Your people will be my people."

So Ruth stayed and followed Naomi's path. They didn't have much, but Ruth and Naomi were able to glean a life together.

And that was enough.

ESTHER

Change and Grow

When the king of Persia selected Esther for his bride, she was not happy. She didn't want to be queen. But she had no choice.

No, Esther didn't want to be queen—but she was good at it. She watched and listened and learned, and the king fell in love with her. All the while, Esther kept an extra-close eye on Haman, the king's right-hand man. He was up to no good.

Her instincts were right. Esther learned that Haman was plotting evil. Shy Esther, who never wanted to be queen, knew she was going to have to stretch to meet the moment. Summoning all her courage, she revealed the truth to the king.

Esther didn't want to be queen, but she was. And because she was a queen, she became a hero.

Do you want to read more
about the characters?
Here is some additional
information.

EVE

Eve was the first woman created and lived in the Garden of Eden alongside her husband, Adam. She is described both as being formed from Adam's rib (Genesis, chapter 2) and as being created alongside Adam "in the image of God" (Genesis 1:27). Adam was commanded by God not to eat fruit from the tree of knowledge, as doing so would result in death. Although Eve was not present at the time of the command, she knew about it. Despite that, she ate the forbidden fruit after the snake in the garden convinced her that it would not kill her but would feed her curiosity. She shared the fruit with Adam, and they were both expelled from Eden. While Eve was ultimately punished for violating God's command, her curiosity opened the door to a more interesting world filled with possibilities.

NOAH

Noah was a righteous man in a world of increasing corruption. He is described as a righteous man who "walked with God" (Genesis, chapter 6), and so when God lamented creation and made plans to destroy the world completely, God established a covenant with Noah and his family. Noah built an ark according to details specified by God and brought aboard pairs of every kind of animal, providing them refuge from the floodwaters. When the deluge was over and the waters receded—more than a year later—Noah and his family emerged from the ark into a world with a set of newly articulated rules of behavior to act as a moral compass. With a rainbow as a symbol, God reaffirmed the covenant and promised never to destroy the earth again.

ABRAHAM

Abraham left his family at God's command and set off to wander to the land of Canaan. With only his wife, Sarah, and a nephew named Lot, Abraham explored a foreign land, struggling through famines, rowdy neighbors, and wars (Genesis, chapters 12–14)— all because God promised him that he would be the founder of a great people. In a vision under the nighttime sky, God told Abraham that his descendants would be as numerous as the stars above (Genesis, chapter 15). But God also put Abraham through trials of faith, including the horrifying command to take his treasured son Isaac and offer him as a sacrifice (Genesis, chapter 22). In the end, his son was spared and the "children of Abraham" continued a covenantal relationship with God.

SARAH

Sarah was the ancestress of all Israel, wife of Abraham, and mother of Isaac. She was unable to conceive a child for most of her life, despite God's promise to Abraham that she would be a "mother of nations" (Genesis 17:16). She gave her maidservant Hagar to Abraham as a surrogate to give birth to Ishmael as an heir for Abraham. When God's promise that she would have a child was repeated (Genesis 18:12), Sarah laughed sarcastically, expressing her doubt. But when she was ninety years old, God's promise was fulfilled and she gave birth to Isaac. His name—meaning "laughter"—reflects the reasonableness of her doubt (Genesis 21:6–7) and her initial reaction of shock and disbelief.

JOSEPH

Joseph was the most loved of his father Jacob's twelve sons, and the only one to whom Jacob gave a special multicolored robe. Already disliked by his brothers because of their father's favoritism, Joseph became hated when he told his brothers he had a dream in which they were bowing down to him. The brothers sold him into slavery and told their father he was dead (Genesis, chapter 37). Taken to Egypt, Joseph wound up in prison after a false accusation, and while there, he interpreted the dreams of two prisoners. Called to the royal court as a dream interpreter, Joseph successfully interpreted Pharaoh's dreams about anticipating seven years of abundant harvest followed by seven years of famine. He told Pharaoh what to do to avoid the worst of the famine, and as a result, Joseph was promoted to chief administrator of Egypt (Genesis, chapters 39–41).

MIRIAM

Miriam was a leader, a musician, a protector, and an innovator. We first meet her on the banks of the Nile River watching over her baby brother Moses, floating in the reeds. When Pharaoh's daughter found her brother, Miriam approached and boldly offered to find a Jewish nursemaid for the baby (Moses's mother, Yocheved). Many years later, after the Israelites crossed the Sea of Reeds and miraculously escaped the Egyptian army (Exodus, chapter 15), Miriam took personal and musical initiative, picked up a timbrel, and led the women in song and dance of praise and celebration. As the sole sister in a family of strong brothers, Miriam emerged as a leader in her own right.

MOSES

Moses was the leader who guided the Israelites out of Egyptian slavery. When he was born, Moses was subject to Pharaoh's decree that all male Israelite babies be killed, and so he was placed in a basket by his mother and floated down the Nile River. There he was found and raised in the Egyptian palace by Pharaoh's daughter. Moses ultimately became a shepherd, and it was while tending his flock in the desert that he encountered God in the form of a burning bush. God called upon Moses to return to Egypt and lead his people from bondage. Despite Moses's initial protestations that he was of "impaired speech" (Exodus 4:10) and not fit for the job, he ultimately took on the challenge, leading the Israelites out of Egypt and into the desert, where they accepted the Torah and formed a religious community. After forty years of wandering in the desert, Moses died without entering the promised land of Israel.

BALAAM

Balaam was a sorcerer who was hired by Balak, king of Moab, to curse the Israelites in order to defeat them in war (Numbers, chapter 22). Along the route, he was met by an angel of the Israelite God, but only Balaam's donkey saw the angel and refused to move. Balaam beat the donkey, and the donkey miraculously spoke to Balaam, whose eyes were then opened to see the angel before him. The angel allowed them to continue but commanded Balaam not to curse the Israelites. He arrived at his destination and incited the anger of King Balak by offering several lengthy and poetic blessings to the Israelite people instead of cursing them.

DEBORAH

Deborah was one of the judges in the Bible during the time of the Israelite settlement of Canaan. She was the only female judge and the only one described as holding court—which she did under a palm tree in the mountains. She convinced Barak to lead in battle against the Canaanites, though he insisted that she go with him, and as she promised, victory was at the hands of a woman (Judges, chapters 4–5). She is known for her wisdom, leadership, and ability to take action. She is one of the few women in the Bible who stands independently of any man in her life and whose importance is uniquely her own.

DAVID

David started out as a humble shepherd and ultimately rose to become the second king of Israel. He gained fame after stepping up and defeating the giant Goliath the Philistine (I Samuel, chapter 17). To bring Goliath down, David used his aim as a slinger and a technique he relied upon to protect his sheep from lions and bears. David became a favorite of King Saul and close friend of Saul's son Jonathan. When Saul and Jonathan were killed in battle against the Philistines (II Samuel, chapter 1), David became king, establishing Jerusalem as his capital. David was also a multitalented musician and poet, with many psalms ascribed to him.

ELIJAH

Elijah was a prophet of Israel in the ninth century BCE. He was a performer of miracles and is depicted as being a leader of a school of prophets. He worked during the reign of King Ahab, who, together with his Phoenician wife, Jezebel, thought people should worship both the God of Israel and the Phoenician god, Baal. Elijah demanded a confrontation with the prophets of Baal on Mount Carmel to prove which was the true God (I Kings, chapter 18). The prophets of Baal cried and screamed and got no reply, but Elijah quietly prayed and was answered with a fire from heaven. As a result of "winning" the contest, Elijah—fearful for his life—runs away to Horeb, where God appears to him in a "still small voice" (I Kings 19:12).

JONAH

Jonah was a prophet in the northern kingdom of Israel in the eighth century BCE. Instead of heeding God's command to go east to Nineveh—a city described as being one of sinners—to get its inhabitants to reform their ways, Jonah fled to the port of Jaffa and boarded a ship heading west to Tarshish, across the Mediterranean Sea. His ship was threatened by a storm, and Jonah was cast overboard when he told the other sailors that the storm was his fault. Swallowed by a large fish, his life was spared (Jonah, chapter 2), and when God again told him to go to Nineveh, Jonah decided he had no choice. After telling the people of Nineveh that they had only forty days to repent, Jonah's life was threatened once again in the dry heat of the desert. From the depths of Jonah's pain and suffering, he came to the realization that he—like all humans and creatures of the world—was dependent upon mercy for survival.

RUTH

Ruth was a Moabite immigrant who, after the death of her husband, moved to Judea with her mother-in-law, Naomi, instead of remaining with her own family and people in Moab. She told Naomi: "Your people are my people, and your God is my God," and refused to leave her despite their poverty and social displacement (Ruth, chapter 1). As a means of support, she went to glean in the fields of others and through this process ultimately became the wife of Boaz, a wealthy relative of her former husband. She and Boaz had a son named Obed, who was the grandfather of King David.

ESTHER

Esther—also known as Hadassah—was a Jewish woman who became queen of Persia and was instrumental in preventing a genocide of her people. She was selected as queen by King Ahasuerus after his first queen, Vashti, was banished for refusing to obey him. Although Esther's Jewish identity was kept secret, the king's chief adviser, Haman, developed a hatred for the Jews and plotted to have them all killed. Together with her relative Mordecai, Esther convinced the king to allow the Jews to defend themselves. Ultimately, Haman was hanged on the gallows that he had prepared for Mordecai, and on the day planned for their destruction, the Jews instead celebrated their survival as a minority community within the empire.

Authors' Note

Shira and Hanoch came to this project from different places. Shira is an educator who has spent many years reading and discussing the Biblical text with family, friends, students, and teachers. Hanoch, on the other hand, is an artist who hasn't read much of the Bible since he dressed up as a Jewish slave in a second-grade play about Passover (although he did enjoy reading many Biblical texts as he was working on this book).

In Hebrew, the act of studying together is called *havruta*, and this book is the product of our joint *havruta*, which was rich and thought-provoking. But it was also playful! We hope you see the playfulness in the portraits of these characters we have grown to love.

Our hope is that at least one person reading this book will be inspired to trust herself like David, forgive himself for feeling embarrassed like Sarah, follow their curiosity like Eve, or go on a journey of exploration like Abraham.

And, of course, there is much more to learn about each character, so perhaps for you, this is the beginning of a lifelong path of personal study, or in *havruta* with a friend.

To my favorite reading buddies, Dalya, Shachar, Amitai, and Aiden

—SHK

To good teachers everywhere

—HP

Farrar Straus Giroux Books for Young Readers
An imprint of Macmillan Publishing Group, LLC
120 Broadway, New York, NY 10271 • mackids.com

Our books may be purchased in bulk for promotional, educational, or business use.
Please contact your local bookseller or the Macmillan Corporate and Premium Sales Department at
(800) 221-7945 ext. 5442 or by email at MacmillanSpecialMarkets@macmillan.com.

Library of Congress Control Number: 2022910017

First edition, 2023
Book design by Neil Swaab
Illustrations photographed by Dima Valerstein
Color separations by Embassy Graphics
Printed in China by RR Donnelley Asia Printing Solutions Ltd.,
Dongguan City, Guangdong Province

ISBN 978-0-374-39010-5 (hardcover)

1 3 5 7 9 10 8 6 4 2